Gann MidPoint Theory : Simplified

Sankar Srinivasan

*Profitable Trading method for Commodity &
Small Cap Shares Intraday*

ANNEXURE

ESSENTIAL QUALIFICATIONS FOR
TRADING

(Gann's Original Writing)

Author: Sankar Srinivasan

*National Stock Exchange of India's
Certified Market Professional & Technical Analyst*

Prepared for Publication by

V.S. PAUL DANIEL ARAVINTH
pauldanielaravinth@gmail.com
(With permission of my father Mr.Sankar Srinivasan)

Published by:

LeoPard Books India
http://LeoPardBooks.com

ISBN-10: 1508950474
ISBN-13: 978-1508950479

Printed by **CreateSpace**, an *Amazon.com* Company

Our Print Books and E-Books are available at
http://amazon.com and all Amazon sites,
http://LeoPardBooks.com, Kobo, Smashwords, Nook
Barnes & Noble, ScribD, Apple and all leading International
online book stores & E-Book stores

Search Terms: "Sankar Srinivasan"

Dedicated to the Legend

William D. Gann

I have just simplified the theory of W.D. Gann. My knowledge is nothing, compared with Gann's

- Sankar Srinivasan

Table of Contents

The Remarkable William D. Gann

John L. Gann, Jr.

If you had been a businessman traveling across Texas in 1891, you might have bought a newspaper and a couple of cigars from a tall, lanky 13-year-old selling them on your train. And as you talked with your fellow travelers about investments, you might have noticed the youth eavesdropping intently on your conversation.

If you had asked him, the boy might have told you his name was Willy and, yes, he was interested in commodities. His dad was a farmer in Angelina County, and just about everyone he knew was as well. They were all concerned about the prices their cotton would bring. And had you inquired whether young Willy also wanted to till the East Texas soil when he got older, he might have said no, he didn't think so: he wanted to be a businessman.

"Well, good luck, young Willy," you might have said. "Maybe you'll have your own business some day, maybe you'll even be famous. Who knows? No one can predict the future."

The young eavesdropper going up and down the aisles of that train was William Delbert

Gann. Was it really true, he might have wondered, that no one can predict the future?

W.D Gann was born on a farm some seven miles outside of Lufkin, Texas, on June 6, 1878. He was the firstborn of 11 children two girls and eight boys of Sam Houston Gann and Susan R. Gann. The Ganns lived in a too small house with no indoor plumbing and with not much of anything else.

They were poor, and young Willy walked the seven miles into Lufkin for three years to go to school. But the work he could do on the farm was more important to the family, so W.D. never graduated from grammar school or attended high school. As the eldest boy, he had a special responsibility, and those years working on the farm may have been the beginning of his lifelong dedication to hard work.

His religious upbringing as a Baptist may also have had something to do with it, for his faith stayed with him throughout his life as well. A few years later W.D. worked in a brokerage in Texarkana and attended business school at night. He married Rena May Smith, and two daughters, Macie and Nora, were born in the first few years of the new twentieth century. W.D. made the fateful move to New York City in 1903 at the age of 25.

Working most likely at a major Wall Street brokerage, W.D. made other changes in his life as well. He divorced his Texas bride and in 1908 at the age of 30 married a 19-year-old colleen named Sarah Hannify. W.D. and Sadie had two children--Velma, born in 1909 and W.D.'s only son, John, who arrived six years later. In addition, Macie and Nora came to live with their father and were raised in New York by their Irish stepmother.

During the First World War the family moved from Manhattan to Brooklyn first to Bay Ridge, then to Flatbush. W.D. reportedly predicted the November 9, 1918, abdication of the Kaiser and the end of the war. But it was after the armistice that the fortunes of the Ganns of Brooklyn took their most dramatic turn. The W.D. that traders know today emerged in the Roaring Twenties.

In 1919 at the age of 41, W.D. Gann quit his job and went out on his own. He spent the rest of his life building his own business. He began publishing a daily market letter, the Supply and Demand Letter. The letter covered both stocks and commodities and provided its readers with annual forecasts. Forecasting was an activity with which W.D. had become fascinated.

The young business prospered, and three years later W.D. Gann became a homeowner, buying a small house on Fenimore Street in his adopted home of Brooklyn. The market letter led to more ambitious publishing. In 1924 W.D.'s first book, Truth of the Stock Tape, was published. A pioneering work on chart reading, it is still regarded by some as the best book ever written on the subject.

An individualist and ambitious hard worker, W.D. self-published Truth through his new Financial Guardian Publishing Company. He personally wrote his own ads to market it and negotiated with bookstores to carry it. Truth as praised by The Wall Street Journal and sold well for years. Some consider it the best of his many books. For a first effort it was a significant accomplishment.

His market forecasts during the twenties were reportedly 85 percent accurate. But W.D. didn't confine his prognostications to prices. It was widely reported he predicted the elections of Wilson and Harding and, indeed, of every president since 1904.

At age 49, W.D. Gann wrote what is perhaps his most unusual book, the 1927 Tunnel Through the Air. It is a prophetic work of fiction, not a genre every Wall Street analyst dabbles in. But W.D. Gann was one of a kind. The book is perhaps best known for having predicted that attack on the United States by Japan and an air war between the two powers. Through Tunnel may have had little to offer investors, it was well-publicized and enhanced its author's growing reputation.

The market in the Twenties seemed to be defying the law of gravity, but W.D. Gann didn't think it could last forever. In his forecast for 1929, he predicted the market would hit new highs until early April, then experience a sharp break, then resume with new highs until September 3. Then it would top and afterward would come the biggest crash in its history. We all know what happened.

W.D. prospered during the Depression, which he predicted would end in 1932. He acquired seats on various commodities exchanges, traded for his own account, wrote Wall Street Stock Selector in 1930 and New Stock Trend Detector in 1936. He continued making remarkably accurate forecasts as well as some less successful ones like the electoral defeat of FDR.

He developed a new interest in investing in Florida real estate. He became a small-scale home-builder in Miami as well as the owner of a block of stores on the Tamiami Trail. He also became airborne. He bought a plane in 1932 so he could fly over crop areas making observations to use in his forecasts. He hired Elinor Smith, a noted 21-year-old aviator, to fly him around. The novelty of his high-flying research-- W.D. was the first to study markets in this way--helped keep him in the spotlight.

W.D.'s son John also went into the securities business in 1936 at the age of 21. A year later he went to work for his dad until in 1941 his Uncle Sam announced he had plans for the young man in Europe. Back in Brooklyn, Sadie had health problems for some time and died at age 53 in 1942. Then after 20 years on Fenimore Street, an aging W.D. Gann moved to Miami for reasons both of health and personal preference. His How to make Profits in Commodities came out the same year.

He kept his business in New York, relying on his long-time personal secretary. In Miami he continued studying the market, trading, real estate investing, and instructing students. The next year at the age of 65, when most are thinking retirement, W.D. decided he'd get married and did, to a much younger woman. Son John worked on W.D.'s business in New York briefly after the war, then left to pursue his own interests in the Industry.

The two differed in their approach to the market. John L. Gann pursued a successful lifetime career with Wall Street's major brokerage housed until his passing in 1984. The post-war years saw W.D. start taking it easier. He published 45 Years in Wall Street in 1949. He sold his business to Joseph Lederer, a fellow student of the market. Around the same time he also separately sold the rights to all his books to Edward Lambert. He continued, however, to study, teach, and trade. He was made an honorary member of the International Mark Twain Society in 1950.

In 1954 he suffered a heart attack. A year later advanced stomach cancer was discovered. The doctors operated, but W.D. failed to recover. He died in June, 1955, at the age of 77. He was buried with his second wife in Green-Wood Cemetery in Brooklyn at a location that looks toward Wall Street. It was a fitting location since he had studied the Street all his adult life.

In 1995, 40 years after his passing, William D. Gann is still talked about, written about, and studied avidly. His books are back in print and are sold by Trader's World and Lambert-Gann Publishing Company. It's an extraordinary testimonial to his work and one that even W.D. couldn't have predicted. Or could he? What lessons might there be in this remarkable man's life?

First is an affirmation of the American Dream. William Delbert Gann of Lufkin, Texas, started with nothing. He and his family had no money, no education, and no prospects. But less than 40 years after overhearing businessmen talk on railroad cars in Texas, W.D. Gann was known around the world.

Second, hard work pays. W.D. rose early, worked late, and approached his business with great energy. Virtually all his education was self-administered. This teacher, writer, and prescient forecaster had a third grade formal education. But he never stopped reading.

Third, unconventional thinking may have its merits. W.D. was intellectually curious to an extraordinary degree. He was unafraid of unorthodox ideas, whether in finance or in other areas of life. He wasn't always right--none of us are--but he dared to pursue a better idea.

Fourth, there may be something to that clean living business after all. A conservative Baptist, W.D. didn't smoke, drink, play cards, or dance. He was serious in demeanour and a conservative dresser, although he lightened up somewhat in his later years. He respected the value of a dollar and was prudent in his personal spending. Not every internationally acclaimed seer would continue to live in a modest house in Brooklyn.

Fifth, faith helps. W.D. studied the Bible all his life. It was his Book of Books. His own last book, The Magic Work, published in 1950, strongly reflects this devotion. And finally, the only lesson for traders I will venture to offer. W.D. never stopped studying the market. Even after his forecasts happened, even after he achieved international acclaim. Although he believed in cycles, he also knew that markets are always changing and that decisions must be made based on today's conditions, not yesterday's.

W.D. might have rested on his laurels. But he kept studying and seeking greater understanding. If he couldn't afford to stop, can any trader afford to do so?

John L. Gann Jr., is the grandson of W.D. Gann. Most of the information in this article comes from W.D. Gann's son, the late John L. Gann, to whom this article is dedicated. The information herein is believed to be correct but no assurance of accuracy is offered.

Gann MidPoint Theory : Simplified

Sankar Srinivasan

Profitable Trading method for Commodity &
Small Cap Shares Intraday

WILLIAM DELBERT GANN

(1878 – 1955)

WHO IS GANN?

In 1902 (at the age of 24), W.D. GANN made his first commodity trade, and makes minimum profit

Over the next 53 years, GANN took over $50,000,000 from the markets

He studied the cause of success and failure in the speculation of other traders

He found that, 90% of traders who enter the markets without knowledge and study usually LOSE in the end.

GANN also LOST a huge amount of money & admitted his trading was based on HOPE, GREED and FEAR (Emotions)

So that, he cautioned all traders about these EMOTIONS in his Books

GANN began to note the periodical recurrence of RISE and FALL in Stocks and Commodities

This led him to conclude that NATURAL LAW was the basis of Market Movements

He Then devoted 10 Years to the study of NATURAL LAW

GANN's Original Writings:

Speculation a Profitable Profession

The Truth of the Stock Tape

The Tunnel Thru the Air

Wall Street Stock Selector

Scientific Stock Forecasting

How to make profits Trading in Puts & Calls

How to make profits Trading in Commodities

45 years in Wall Street

WHO IS GANN?

In GANN's time there were no calculators. He used Graph Sheet for Charting.

In his early trading, he made 1000s of Dollars

But, by listening to FALSE rumours and other people's ideas, he also lost 1000s of Dollars

He used many methods for forecasting

Square of 9 chart
Square of 144 chart
Hexagon chart
Square of 90
Square of 52
360 degree circle chart
Midpoint trading strategy
And many more…………

GANN MidPoint Theory

Market tasks of a Trader in Stock, Commodity and Forex Markets

BUY & SELL

Most Traders are BUYing in BEAR market

& SELLing in BULL market

Why this mistakes…..???

Wrong Entry & Exit Areas

Emotional Trades

Trades without any decision, Target

Trades by Rumours

Trades by Tips from someone

Trades Copied from someone

Over Trade

Trading is simple……

When we are able to find correct entry area

When we are able to find correct exit area

When we are able to trade sufficient volume with sufficient margin

How to find exact Entry Area?

With help of Broker Recommendations

Expert Tips

(Both assures Dependability & Expense)

Technical Analysis Software

(Expensive)

So, we need a Theory

We need a theory for a successful trading

Anyone can make new theory for stock market

Or, follow a theory invented by Market Experts

GANN Theory
Fibonacci Theory
Dow Theory
Elliott Wave Theory
and many more…. theories available

WHY WE CHOOSE GANN THEORY???

GANN Theory is easy to understand

Anyone can use without expert knowledge

We are able to find exact entry and exit areas

We may expect near about 90% Accuracy

GANN MIDPOINT THEORY
Calculations

Price Squaring Method

GANN MidPoint Theory Calculations

GOLDEN RULES:

Only for Day Trading. Not for positional or Delivery trade.

Use this for Commodity, Stock and Indices. IT IS GIVING BETTER RESULTS FOR SMALL CAP SHARES

Don't use it for Option and Forex trading

Take Day High, Day Low and Current Price at ANY POINT OF TIME during market hours

After calculation, you can find Buy area OR Sell area, Targets and Stop Loss. Use these data for trading.

If BUY or SELL area achieves, involve trading and close the position

Use MULTIPLE TIMES for a Scrip

Use the theory in virtual trade for few days, before real trade

All above rules are important

First Trade by using GANN's MIDPOINT

(Virtual data)

DOW JONES FUTURES

Intra Day High Price   –   7500

Intra Day Low Price   –   7450

Current Price   –   7485

1) Add High Price with Low Price and divide by 2.   It is called MidPoint

= (7500+7450)/2

= 14950/2

= 7475 is MidPoint

2) Find Termination Price Range (TPR) (This is ideal for finding Target)

If Current Price is greater than Midpoint, Formula is

$$TPR = Midpoint + (sqrt(high\text{-}midpoint)+2)^2$$

If Current Price is Less than Midpoint,

Formula is

$$TPR = Midpoint - (sqrt(high\text{-}midpoint)-2)^2$$

If Current Price is equal to Midpoint =

No Formula (means NO TRADE)

In our example, Current Price 7485 is greater than MidPoint 7475. So, formula is

$TPR = Midpoint + (sqrt(high\text{-}midpoint)+2)^2$
$TPR = 7475 + (sqrt(7500\text{-}7475)+2)^2$
$TPR = 7475 + (sqrt(25)+2)^2$
$TPR = 7475 + (5+2)^2$
$TPR = 7475 + (7)^2$
$TPR = 7475 + 49$
TPR = 7524

3) TRADE DECISION

If TPR is greater than MidPoint, BUY otherwise SHORT SELL

In our example, TPR 7524 is greater than MidPoint 7475. So, you have to BUY

BUY ENTRY $= (HIGH+Midpoint)/2$

$= (7500+7475)/2$

$= 14975/2 = 7487.50$

= BUY AT 7487.50

TARGET $= (HIGH + TPR)/2$

$= (7500+7524)/2$

$= 15024/2$

= TARGET 7512

STOP LOSS **= MIDPOINT (7475)**

First Trade by using GANN's MIDPOINT

(Virtual data)

DOW JONES FUTURES

Intra Day High Price　– 7500

Intra Day Low Price　– 7450

Current Price　　　　　– 7465

1) Add High Price with Low Price and divide by 2. It is called MidPoint

$= (7500+7450)/2$

$= 14950/2$

= 7475 is MidPoint

2) Find Termination Price Range (TPR) (This is ideal for finding Target)

If Current Price is greater than Midpoint, Formula is

$$TPR = Midpoint + (sqrt(high\text{-}midpoint)+2)2$$

If Current Price is Less than Midpoint,

Formula is

$$TPR = Midpoint - (sqrt(high\text{-}midpoint)\text{-}2)2$$

If Current Price is equal to Midpoint =

No Formula (means NO TRADE)

In our example, Current Price 7465 is LESS than MidPoint 7475. So, formula is

$TPR = Midpoint - (sqrt(high\text{-}midpoint)\text{-}2)^2$
$TPR = 7475 - (sqrt(7500\text{-}7475)\text{-}2)^2$
$TPR = 7475 - (sqrt(25)\text{-}2)^2$
$TPR = 7475 - (5\text{-}2)^2$
$TPR = 7475 - (3)^2$
$TPR = 7475 - 9$
TPR = 7466

3) TRADE DECISION

= If TPR is greater than MidPoint, BUY otherwise SHORT SELL

In our example, TPR 7466 is less than MidPoint 7475. So, you have to SELL

SELL ENTRY   = (LOW+Midpoint)/2

          = (7450+7475)/2

          = 14925/2

          = SELL AT 7462.50

TARGET   = (LOW + TPR)/2

          = (7450+7466)/2

          = 14916/2

          = TARGET 7458

STOP LOSS   =   MIDPOINT (7475)

*** Target difference depends on gap between high and low prices ***

Enter BUY or SELL (Anyone Trade)

Use multiple times per day per scrip

Use trailing stop loss to maximize the profit

In my personal experience, it is giving profit for 7 to 8 trades out of 10

Manual calculation is time consuming. So, please kindly send scan copy or email copy of bill of this book, to petra.srini@gmail.com

I will send a excel sheet calculator. In that excel sheet calculator, you just enter high, low & current prices. It will generate entry, target and stop loss within fraction of seconds

W.D. Gann's Trading Rules

- ✓ Don't enter a trade, if you are unsure of the trend. Never buck the trend
- ✓ When in doubt, get out, and don't get in when in doubt
- ✓ Only trade active markets
- ✓ Distribute your risk equally among different markets
- ✓ Never limit your orders. Trade at the market
- ✓ Don't close trades without a good reason
- ✓ Never trade to scalp a profit
- ✓ Never average a loss
- ✓ Never get out of the market because you have lost patience or get in because you are anxious from waiting
- ✓ Avoid taking small profits and large losses

- ✓ Never cancel a stop loss after you have placed the trade
- ✓ Avoid getting in and out of the market too often
- ✓ Be willing to make money from both sides of the market
- ✓ Never buy or sell just because the price is low or high
- ✓ Pyramiding should be accomplished once it has crossed resistance levels and broken zones of distribution
- ✓ Pyramid issues that have a strong trend
- ✓ Never hedge a losing position
- ✓ Never change your position without a good reason
- ✓ Avoid trading after long periods of success or failure
- ✓ Don't try to guess tops or bottoms.
- ✓ Don't follow a blind man's advice
- ✓ Reduce trading after the first loss; never increase
- ✓ Avoid getting in wrong and out wrong; or getting in right and out wrong. This is making a doubt mistake

A SINCERE REQUEST

Thank you for reading this book. If you have any doubts on the calculations, please feel free to contact the Author by Mobile/WhatsApp or by email

Contact Details

Sankar Srinivasan
Mobile/WhatsApp: +91 90 4240 4390
Petra.srini@gmail.com

OTHER SIMPLIFIED BOOKS BY ME

GANN Square of 9
GANN MidPoint Theory
GANN Angle Theory
Fibonacci Retracement

Available at amazon.com and leopardbooks.com

ANNEXURE

ESSENTIAL QUALIFICATIONS FOR TRADING

William D. Gann

ESSENTIAL QUALIFICATIONS FOR TRADING

- *William D. Gann*

PATIENCE

Patience is a virtue, especially in the stock market. Acquire it if you can. You must have patience to wait for the right opportunity to come, and not be overanxious and get in too soon. Once you buy or sell a stock and it starts moving in your favor, you must have patience to hold it until there is a good reason or sufficient cause for closing the trade. Never close a trade just because you have a profit; do not become impatient and get out for no real reason.

Every act, either in opening or closing a trade, must have a sound basic cause behind it. Hopes and fears must be eliminated. There is no use selling a stock because you fear it is going down, nor buying it because you hope it is going up. Look at your charts and see which way the trend points and follow it. If no definite trend is shown, use patience and wait.

NERVE

Nerve is just as essential as patience; in fact, nerve is the equal of capital. In getting my experience, I have been broke over 40 times, i. e., I have lost all of my money, but there never has been a time yet when I lost my nerve. Years ago, when I was experimenting and working on methods for forecasting the market, I would get in the market wrong and lose all my working capital, but I never let it get my "goat." I studied very carefully how I made the mistake and what the cause of the loss was. In this way, I profited by every mistake and loss, and was enabled to perfect my method of forecasting and trading so that I could make a success. Looking backward brings nothing but regrets. I always believe in facing the future with nerve and hope. But let the nerve and the hope be based on some sound principle that will prevent costly mistakes of the past.

During my career I have seen many traders who had made one mistake after another and suffered severe losses, and still had some capital to work with but when an opportunity appeared, they lacked the nerve to act. In cases of this kind, the nerve would have been more valuable than capital.

KNOWLEDGE

In the early part of my career I made some great success, and what might be called lucky strikes. I made a lot of money easily and then I spent or lost it easily. But I did not give up or lose my nerve. I always figured that I was a better man after each reverse, because I had acquired experience.

Experience is the only school to learn in and the burnt child is the one who knows the pain from having put his fingers in the fire. Mistakes are all right and hard to avoid. They are good for us, because if we profit by them, they prove valuable. But it is wrong to make the same mistake the second time. Therefore, use every mistake as a stepping stone to progress; analyze each mistake you make and the cause of every loss, in order to avoid repeating the same error in future.

With each experience I had, good or bad, I accumulated knowledge, and after all, knowledge is the greatest power of all, for capital will always come to knowledge. Several years ago a brokerage failure occurred suddenly and unexpectedly, and I lost all of my money. To the ordinary man's way of figuring I was broke, but as a friend of mine expressed it at the time, "He may be without cash, but the knowledge that he has of the stock market is worth hundreds of thousands of dollars and in a short time he will turn that knowledge into cash."

I did come back quickly in a few months' time on a small capital, because I had a greater knowledge of the stock market than ever before, and knowing, by experience, that I had a method based upon mathematical science which could be depended upon to forecast the stock market, I had the nerve to pyramid and press the market hard when my science showed that I was on the right side. What would have been the result had I been without knowledge and only filled with hope? I would have stayed broke, as other traders do who follow the fairy phantom of "hope" in Wall Street trading.

HEALTH AND REST

Good health is essential to success in any line. It is one of the great assets for success in the speculative market. At least twice a year a man should close up all of his trades, get entirely out of the market, and go away for a vacation or stay away from the market and rest up. Let your mind rest and your judgment get clear. The man who continually sticks to any business too long without a rest or change gets his judgment warped. He gets in a rut and sees things from a one-sided point of view.

When you are in the market on either side, it is but human nature for you to hope that it will go your way, and you, therefore, give greater weight to any event that seems to indicate a favorable move to your side. When you are out of the market, you are able to see things as they really are, and judge the market without a distorted view, with hope and fear eliminated. Traders who are continually in the market day in and day out and never allow any time to elapse between trades, sooner or later lose all their money.

I know one trader who follows scientific forecasting and makes a success. He never makes more than five or six trades in the year. If he buys stocks during the winter or early spring for a rise, and the advance materializes as he expected, he sells out and takes his profits. Then he leaves the market alone, sometimes for several months. In the summer, if he sees indications of a bull or a bear market starting, he gets in again, and if the market moves his way, he may follow it up and pyramid for several months.

When he gets an indication that the end is near, he closes up his trades, takes his profits, and like the wild geese, wends his way to the sunny South. Sometimes he stays all winter in Florida, hunting and fishing; then goes over to Hot Springs, Arkansas, takes a course of baths; returns to Wall Street in good health and fit for another tilt with the Bulls and Bears.

He makes a specialty of trading in certain favorite stocks. He studies them closely and watches for certain signs that he considers almost infallible. When these signs come, he acts. He does not hurry until the time comes, but when it does, there is no hesitation -- he buys or sells. He keeps cool, calm and collected, and waits for the time to open or close a trade.

Another thing he never does is to expect any fixed amount of profits or set any specific time for getting out. I have often seen him make a trade and it would go against him. He would get out and say, "Well, I guess I'll go back to my office and watch them for awhile." Sometimes it would be days or weeks before he made another trade, but when he did, it was based on some good sound reason, and 90 per cent of the time the second trade proved a winner. But suppose he had held the first trade he made and hoped it would move his way. His judgment, being biased, would have become more unreliable all the time. There is nothing like being out of the market and looking them over from an impartial viewpoint. When there is no definite trend, stay out, watch and wait, and your patience will be rewarded.

W. D. Gann, *Truth of the Stock Tape*

WHEN A MAN's TREND CHANGES

- *William D. Gann*

Man's seasonal trend changes just as the market and he has his good and bad cycles. By keeping a record of your own trades, you can determine when your trend is changing one way or the other. I have been able to make as many as 200 consecutive trades without a loss. When I started the campaign, I did not believe I could make 50 trades without a loss, but I did continue to make perfect trades and close every trade with a profit, until I had made 200 trades. This run of luck or up trend that I was in, had run for some time. If I had no way to forecast it, what sign should I watch to tell when the tide had turned against me and I should get out and wait? The first indication that something was wrong would be the first trade on which I made a loss. I remember that it was a small loss, around $100.

On the next trade I had a loss of over $500. This showed that my trend was changing and turning against me, whether due to bad judgment, ill health, tired nerves, or other causes. If I had been wise, I would have quit and kept all of my profits. I made the third trade and as most traders do, went into the market on a larger scale. This trade soon showed a loss of $5,000 and I did not take the loss quickly. The result was that I continued to make a series of losses until the banks closed in November, 1907, and I could not get any more money out of the banks. I was forced to close out all of my commitments with my brokers and take a big loss, because I was bucking my own trend. My period of good luck had run out, and I was trading in a period which should have been for rest, recreation, and gaining knowledge instead of trying to make more money which I did not need. The banks were unable to pay currency for several months, and I could not get any money to speculate with. I put in my time studying and figuring on the market and found out what caused my mistake and the losses.

I started trading again in the Spring of 1908, and should have had some rule to tell me when my trend had turned in my favor. I began to trade in Wheat and the first three trades I made showed profits. This was a sign that luck was with me and I should press it. I then started a campaign buying Cotton and followed the market right on up, pyramiding at the same time that [legendary trader Jesse] Livermore made his first successful corner in July Cotton. I made a large amount of money.

I could give you many more examples of my experiences of profits and losses but one rule that every trader should watch and follow is, just as soon as he makes two or three wrong trades after a long series of profits, he should quit the market and take a rest. Get away from the market. Allow plenty of time for his judgment to clear up. Then, when he thinks he is right again, make a start on a small trade.

If the first trade goes against him, he should quit again and stay away. Then, when he starts again, if his first two or three trades show profits, he can press his luck and expect a period of success until he sees another sign that the tide has turned against him, when he must again get out of the market.

I have always made the biggest profits after I have remained out of the market for a long period of time and have always made the biggest losses after I have been in a campaign in the market for a long period of time. No man can trade heavily in the market without having a strain on his nervous system, and when his nerves begin to give way and his health is below normal, his judgment gets bad and he begins to make losses.

There is no use in staying in, holding on and hoping, when things start going against you. Take your loss quickly and get out. You will make money by staying out of the market and waiting for an opportunity when the market is right, your physical condition good and your mind at its best. To beat the stock market is a battle of wits. Your mind must be active, keen and alert. You must be able to change your mind and act quickly. When you find that your mind gets sluggish and you cannot act quickly, you are in no position to be in the market.

I have been connected with brokerage offices and have known the position of a large number of traders. I have seen the market go against them for days and weeks. Gradually they would start getting out, but a few would be very stubborn and hold on. I call it stubbornness; they called it nerve, but it is not nerve which makes a man hold on when the market is going against him. It is hope and stubbornness. Nerve will not outlast a market that is going against you, and even if the nerve does last, your money will not last to continue to buck the trend. Traders usually talk with each other in the boardroom. When all but two or three have gotten out with losses, they will talk with each other and say they are going to put up more margin, stick it out until the turn comes.

Finally, there is one left, and he will say that he is not going to sell out on the bottom but will see it through. Finally, his hope gives way to despair and he puts in an order to sell at a price on a rally.

The market fails to reach his selling price. Then he changes the price for several days and misses it, and the market continues to go lower. Finally, he gives an order to sell out at the market. That was my signal to buy. I would then buy at the market and invariably made profits. This shows that the *trader nearly always does the wrong thing* at *the wrong time* after he has held on for a long period of time. This proves that the man who has health, money, nerve and knowledge and stays out of the market until the psychological moment can always make big profits.

Some man who has made and lost a lot of money betting on the races wrote the following poem:

> "The time to pitch in is when others discouraged show signs of tire"

> "The battle is fought in the home stretch and won twixt the flag and the wire."

It is the ability to act and begin at a time when others see no hope that helps to make a success in speculation. When everything looks the bluest and nobody can see a ray of hope, it is time to buy good stocks. When the pot is boiling and everybody is optimistic, with not a cloud in the sky, it is time to sell. Hope, in one case, has wrecked and ruined judgment and, at the other extreme, fear has caused loss of hope, loss of judgment, and through discouragement, traders sell out on the bottom and many of them go short. This is the wise fool's opportunity and the man who has nerve to weighed in at these extremes will make money.

The man with money who is out of the market and is studying and watching his charts can see these opportunities at the extremes and take advantage of them.

FEAR Vs KNOWLEDGE

Fear is one of the great causes of losses in Wall Street. In fact, fear is the cause of most all of our troubles and misfortunes in life. What causes fear? It is ignorance or lack of knowledge. The Bible says, "Ye shall know the truth and the truth shall make you free." The truth is knowledge whether it is scientific or otherwise, and when a man has knowledge, he sees and knows and does not fear.

With knowledge, he does not hope, because he knows what will happen, and does not hope or fear what will happen.

Why does a man sell out stocks at the lowest point? It is because he fears they will go lower. If he knew that they were at the lowest point, he would have no fear, and instead of selling, he would buy. The same applies at the top. Why does a man buy at the highest point or cover shorts at the highest point? Because he has lost hope and fears they are going higher. If he had knowledge, he would have no fear and would use good judgment. To succeed, hope and fear must be eliminated, and the only way to eliminate these two imposters is to get as much knowledge as you can.

WHY TRADERS DO NOT SELL OUT STOCKS AT HIGH LEVELS

In every bull market many traders have enormous profits, but fail to get out at the right time. They let stocks decline and sometimes wipe out 50 to 100 points' profit before selling out. There must be a reason for this. We have heard much talk of Wall Street psychology and some writers have said that the 1929 Wall Street panic was due to mob psychology. This is largely true, but mob psychology would not have caused the panic if previously mob psychology had not caused the big bull market when everybody bought, got over-optimistic and failed to get out with big profits.

The following incident, which actually happened, illustrates why people do not sell out stocks when they have big profits. A gentleman who I have known for many years bought U. S. Steel around 80 in 1921. He held it and received the stock dividend of 40 per cent in 1927. Then, when the new stock declined to 111 1/4, he bought some when it rallied to 115, and held all of this stock until it advanced to 261 3/4 in September, 1929.

Long before the stock crossed 175, he talked about selling it at 200, but when it crossed 200, he decided that it was going to 250, and waited to sell at that price. About the time that U. S. Steel advanced to 250 this man met a friend of mine and said to him, "What does Gann think of Steel now?"

My friend replied, "Gann says that the market is going to be top around the end of August and he is going to go short of U. S. Steel."

This man said, "I hear that U. S. Steel is going to 300 or higher and then be split up 4 for 1, and then I am going to sell out."

After U. S. Steel sold at 150 in November, 1929, this man came into the office of my friend who said to him, "Mr. H., did you sell your U. S. Steel above $250?"

He answered, "No, I did not sell it, and I have it yet."

My friend said, "Why on earth didn't you sell out when you had such big profits?"

The man replied, "Well, you know they have a way of hypnotizing you and putting you to sleep when stocks are up near top, then you don't wake up and realize what has happened until they are down near the bottom and it is too late to sell."

This man's statement shows that people do get hypnotized and do not realize what has happened or what is going to happen until it is too late, which is one of the reasons why they do not sell out stocks at high levels. If investors and traders would only learn to follow up their profits with a stop loss order, which would get them out with a good part of their profits when the decline starts, they would be much better off.

What was the use of this man allowing U. S. Steel, which he had bought at the right time, to decline over 100 points and wipe out the biggest part of his profits? Of course, after Steel was down 20 points he did not believe that it would decline 80 or 90 points more; if he had, he would have sold out. Remember, it is not what you believe, think or hope that counts, but it is what the market does, therefore you must have some rule to protect your profits, once you have made them. I know of no better automatic protection than the stop loss order.

THE WISE FOOL

The cock-sure trader, who thinks he knows it all, follows tips and inside information. He condemns what he does not understand and never makes progress because he thinks he knows it all. Such a man calls a follower of science and charts, a fool, but the follower of charts is a wise fool.

I quote from *Ist Corinthians 2:13-14*: "Which things also we speak, not in the words which man's wisdom teacheth, but which the Holy Ghost teacheth; comparing spiritual things with spiritual. But the natural man receiveth not the things of the spirit of God, for they are foolishness unto him, neither can he know them, because they are spiritually discerned."

The natural or average man considers science as applied to the stock market foolishness and condemns charts because he does not understand how to read them. To him they are foolishness because he does not know the rules by which to read them. He has not had years of experience and has not been trained to properly read or accurately determine the future course of stocks. The successful trader is the man who knows that he does not know it all and who is always trying to learn more. When once a man decides he knows it all about the stock market, he is doomed to failure. When activity decreases, stagnation sets in and when a man no longer continues to learn he goes backward, not forward. A successful man must have a plan and rules and follow them.

W. D. Gann, *Wall Street Stock Selector*

About Author

Sankar Srinivasan

National Stock Exchange of India's Certified Market
Professional
Licentiate of Insurance Institute of India
Acupuncturist
Left Political Activist & Writer

Sankar Srinivasan is a Technical Analyst, living in
Madurai City of Tamil Nadu State in India. He is
having more than 10 years experience in Stocks,
Fuures, Commodities and Currency Trading. He has
conducted various training programs in Technical

Analysis and Gann theories. He is s Certified Market
Professional of National Stock Exchange of India

A OFFER TO YOU

Dear Reader

Post your reviews about this book in Amazon or other sales channel, wherever you bought the book. Send the link to petra.srini@gmail.com, and get

FIBONACCI RETRACEMENT : SIMPLIFIED E-Book, absolutely FREE (worth $9.99)

FIBONACCI RETRACEMENT is a simple and wonderful mathematical tool for successful FOREX & Small Cap Trading. No Technical Analysis knowledge needed

Attention: Book Sellers
For Volume Discount or Business Enquiry,
Please contact us by email

Petra.srini@gmail.com

FOLLOWING PAGES ARE
INTENTIONALLY LEFT BLANK FOR
NOTES